BUILT FOR SPEED
AIRCRAFT

IAN GRAHAM

RSVP

RAINTREE
STECK-VAUGHN
PUBLISHERS
A Steck-Vaughn Company

Austin, Texas

Published by Raintree Steck-Vaughn Publishers, an imprint of
Steck-Vaughn Company

Editors: Stephanie Bellwood, Kathy DeVico
Designer: Dave Goodman
Series design: Helen James
Illustrator: Tom Connell (Diagram p. 17 by Kevin Lyles)
Picture researcher: Diana Morris
Consultants: Lindsay Peacock, Ann Robinson

Library of Congress Cataloging-in-Publication Data
Graham, Ian, 1953–
        Aircraft/Ian Graham.
            p.   cm. — (Built for speed)
        Includes index.
        ISBN 0-8172-4220-1 (hardcover)
        ISBN 0-8172-8072-3 (softcover)
        1. Airplanes—Juvenile literature.
    [1. Airplanes.] I. Title.   II. Series.
    TL547.G73   1999
    629.13 — dc21   97-48522
    CIP   AC

Printed in Hong Kong
Bound in the United States
1 2 3 4 5 6 7 8 9 0 02 01 00 99 98

Picture acknowledgments:
Airbus Industrie: 9. Air France/TRH Pictures: 15. British Aerospace/TRH Pictures: 16.British
Airways/TRH Pictures: 26. Ian Graham: 28t, 29t. Military Picture Library: 25.NASA/TRH Pictures:
13, 14, 20. E. Nevill/TRH Pictures: 6, 18. Northrop Grumman Corp/TRH Pictures: 28b. Quadrant
Picture Library: 11, 21, 23, 24, 27. Rolls-Royce plc: 8, 10. Sikorsky/TRH Pictures: 22. TRH
Pictures: 19. USAF/TRH Pictures: 17, 29b.U.S. National Archives/TRH Pictures: 12.
U.S. Navy/TRH Pictures: 7.

Words in **bold** are explained in the glossary.

Contents

The Quest for Speed   4

Designing for Speed   6

On the Drawing Board   8

Will It Work?   10

Engine Power   12

Supersonic Flight   14

Fast and Furious   16

Flying to Win   18

Blasting into Space   20

Spinning Wings   22

Staying in Control   24

Record-Breakers   26

Shaping the Future   28

Glossary   30

Index   32

The Quest for Speed

Ever since the first person climbed on a horse and galloped into the distance, people have been finding new ways of traveling farther and faster. In 1903 the Wright brothers made the world's first powered flight. Since then we have found ways to fly halfway around the world at twice the **speed of sound** and double the height of Mount Everest in just a few hours. Today aircraft design is still changing rapidly.

▲ The first airplane
The first successful airplane was the Wright Flyer, built by Orville and Wilbur Wright. On December 17, 1903, the plane took off under its own power for the first time. It flew 98 feet (30 m) and reached a speed of 30 mph (48 kph).

◄ The first fighters
When World War I broke out in 1914, fast, well-armed fighter planes were quickly designed. One of the fastest fighters was the Spad 7. It flew at 130 mph (210 kph).

▲ Super fighter
The Supermarine Spitfire was one of the most famous fighters of World War II. It was small and light, and could fly at almost 370 miles per hour (600 kph). The Spitfire could climb, dive, turn, and attack much faster than many enemy planes.

▲ Speedy airliner
The Douglas DC-3 was one of the most popular American airliners of the 1930s. It transported **cargo**, military supplies, and passengers. The DC-3 was so useful that more than 13,000 were built. It flew up to 218 mph (350 kph).

▼ The first jet airliner

The British De Havilland DH-106 Comet was the first jet airliner. This amazing aircraft was built in 1949. It had a top speed of 500 miles per hour (790 kph), and it could fly twice as fast as other airliners.

▼ Jumbo-sized planes

The largest passenger planes are Boeing 747 Jumbo Jets, designed in the early 1960s. The largest is the 747-400. It weighs up to 871,000 pounds (395,000 kg) and flies at a speed of 610 mph (980 kph).

▲ Faster than sound

Concorde is the fastest airliner in the world. It flies faster than sound. In fact, Concorde **cruises** at twice the speed of sound. An aircraft that flies faster than sound is called **supersonic**.

Designing for Speed

The shape of an aircraft is a vital part of its design. An aircraft pushes air aside as it flies along. At the same time, air pushes back and slows down the aircraft. This is called air resistance, or **drag**. The faster an aircraft tries to fly, the more air resistance there is. Fast planes are shaped like darts so that they can cut through the air at high speeds. Smoothing out an aircraft's shape so that it slips through the air easily is called streamlining.

▼ Folding undercarriage

Most aircraft have a retractable **undercarriage**. After takeoff, doors in the **fuselage** and wings open to let the wheels retract, or fold up, inside the plane. Then the doors close and form a smooth, streamlined surface.

Boeing 767
jet airliner

Dash 7
airliner

▲ Swept back for speed

Slow planes such as the Dash 7 airliner have wings that stick straight out. Fast jet airliners like the Boeing 767 have wings angled backward to be more streamlined. The wings of supersonic planes like the Dassault Rafale fighter are swept back so far that they form a triangular shape called a **delta wing**.

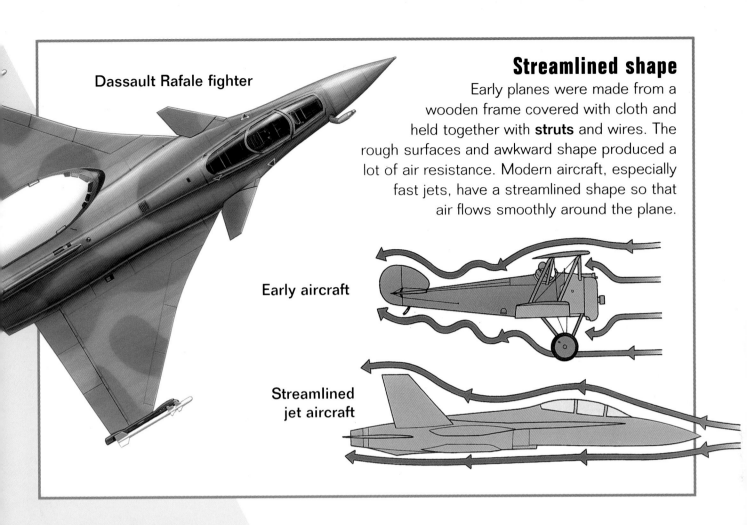

Dassault Rafale fighter

Streamlined shape

Early planes were made from a wooden frame covered with cloth and held together with **struts** and wires. The rough surfaces and awkward shape produced a lot of air resistance. Modern aircraft, especially fast jets, have a streamlined shape so that air flows smoothly around the plane.

Early aircraft

Streamlined jet aircraft

Engine design

Small, light aircraft with piston engines can fly up to 370 mph (600 kph). Heavier and faster planes need a more powerful engine. Airliners and fighters often have jet engines. The fastest jet aircraft fly at 1,240–1,865 miles per hour (2,000–3,000 kph).

Piston engine plane

Jet engine plane

▲ Increasing the power

Concorde and most fighters use jet engines with **afterburners**. When the pilot turns on the afterburners, fuel is sprayed into the fiery hot gases streaming out of the engine. The fuel burns and produces extra power for takeoff or **acceleration**.

On the Drawing Board

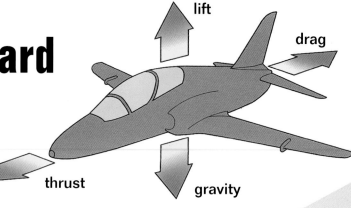

An aircraft is a complicated machine. It is built from thousands of parts made from materials such as metal, plastic, glass, and rubber. Modern aircraft are designed with the help of computers. This is called computer-aided design. The computer can show a picture of the whole aircraft or any part of it, and turn it around so that the designer can see it from every angle. The BAe Hawk 200 was designed by computer. It is light and extremely fast.

▲ Forces of flight

There are four forces that act on an aircraft when it flies. **Gravity** pulls it down, so wings or spinning rotor blades lift it. Air resistance, or drag, slows down the aircraft, so engines produce **thrust** to push it forward.

BAe Hawk 200

◄ Computer-aided design

Computers speed up the process of designing an aircraft. Designers change and experiment with parts of an aircraft quickly and easily using a computer. The aircraft is changed and improved many times before it is built.

Eject!

An ejection seat can blast a pilot
to safety in less than three seconds.
When the pilot pulls the firing handle,
the seat is fired out of the cockpit
and pushed clear of the plane by rockets.
The seat falls away, and the
pilot lands by parachute.

FAST FACTS

Fast aircraft fly at such high speeds that air rushing past
heats them up. Designers of the fastest planes have to
choose a strong metal, such as **titanium**, or the planes
might become so hot that they melt!

On the production line ➤
Computers control the process
of making aircraft parts and
building the finished aircraft.
Many pieces are
welded together,
and computers
make sure that
nothing goes wrong.
It is a quick and
efficient production line.

Will It Work?

New aircraft are tested to make sure that they are safe before they are given to air forces or airlines. Testing begins even before the aircraft is built. Computers and models show how each part of the aircraft will work during flight. When the aircraft is built, test pilots fly it to make sure there are no unexpected problems and that it flies exactly as its designers planned.

◄ Computer testing
Computers draw colorful pictures of the new aircraft to show how parts will move in flight. Designers can see which parts have to be strongest. This computer image is an engine fan.

McDonnell Douglas aircraft testing new engines

◄ Flying test beds
Sometimes a part designed for a new aircraft is tested by building it into another aircraft. An aircraft used in this way is called a flying test bed. It is a good way of testing new engines or a different wing shape.

◄ Early days

In the early days of aircraft, the only way to test a new plane was to fly it. Early planes were slower than most modern cars, but they were still very dangerous to fly. The controls were hard to use, and the pilot had no protection at all.

Lockheed Martin
F-22 model

◄ Wind tunnel

A model of the airplane is tested in a **wind tunnel**. Air blown by huge **propellers** flows past the model, and computers record how it moves. This tells scientists and engineers how the real aircraft will fly.

Mach numbers

The speed of fast aircraft is not always measured in miles per hour. The speed of sound is called Mach 1. The fastest planes can fly at more than Mach 3, three times the speed of sound. The Mach speed system was named after Ernst Mach (1838–1916), a scientist who studied how air flows around objects moving at high speeds.

Sepecat Jaguar: Mach 1.6

McDonnell Douglas
F-15 Eagle: Mach 2.5

Boeing 747: Mach 0.9

Engine Power

Fast aircraft need powerful engines to propel them through the air. Concorde and a few of the fastest fighters are powered by a jet engine called a turbojet. Most airliners and fighters are powered by a jet engine called a turbofan. All jet engines work in the same way. Air is sucked inside and heated by burning fuel. The heat makes the air expand so that it rushes out of the engine as a jet of hot gas.

Panavia Tornado

Rocket-powered fighter ➤
The Messerschmitt Me-163 Komet was the first rocket-powered fighter. In 1941 it broke the world air speed record when it flew at 625 miles per hour (1,004 kph). Komets were dangerous planes to fly because they had a habit of exploding when landing!

⋏ Flying to the limit
The X-15 was a U.S. rocket plane that flew to the limits of the Earth's **atmosphere** many times in the 1960s. Its rocket engine boosted it to speeds of more than 4,350 miles per hour (7,000 kph). The design of the X-15 was used to help build the space shuttle.

Burning fuel ➤
Fuel inside an engine can only burn when **oxygen** is added. Jet engines suck in oxygen from the air, but in space there is no air to use. This means that rockets have to carry their own oxygen supply.

Rocket flies upward.

fuel

oxygen

hot gases out

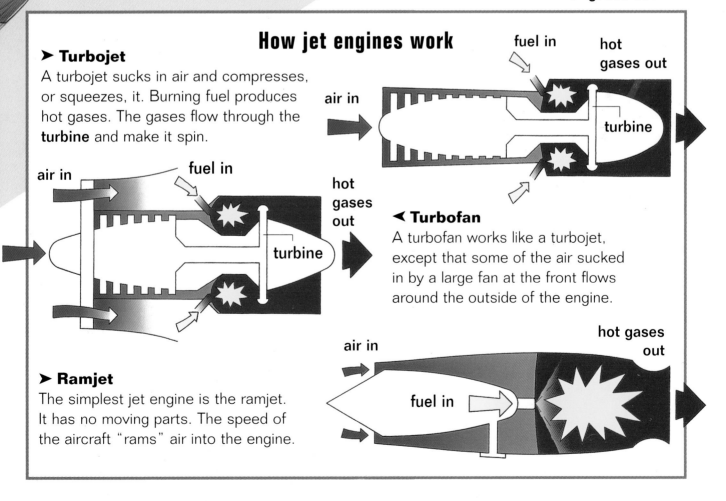

How jet engines work

➤ Turbojet
A turbojet sucks in air and compresses, or squeezes, it. Burning fuel produces hot gases. The gases flow through the **turbine** and make it spin.

air in

fuel in

hot gases out

turbine

air in

fuel in

hot gases out

turbine

◄ Turbofan
A turbofan works like a turbojet, except that some of the air sucked in by a large fan at the front flows around the outside of the engine.

➤ Ramjet
The simplest jet engine is the ramjet. It has no moving parts. The speed of the aircraft "rams" air into the engine.

air in

fuel in

hot gases out

Supersonic Flight

Aircraft that can fly faster than the speed of sound have a streamlined shape to help them fly at high speeds. The wings are thin with sharp edges and swept back so much that they sometimes join the tail to form a delta wing. The body of the aircraft is slim, its engines are narrow, and its nose ends in a sharp point. The aircraft speeds through the air without wasting fuel and engine power in overcoming air resistance.

Eurofighter EFA-2000

What is a sonic boom?

When an aircraft flies faster than sound, air in front of it does not move aside fast enough. It piles up in front of the plane and forms a shock wave, which is like the wave of water that builds up in front of a ship. The shock wave spreads out like ripples of water. When it reaches the ground, it makes a loud, booming noise. This is called a sonic boom. You can hear it as the aircraft passes over your head.

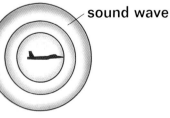

sound wave

Slower than sound

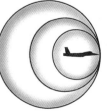

At the speed of sound

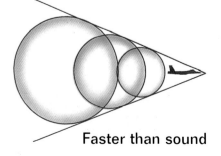

Faster than sound

◄ A supersonic first

The first plane to fly faster than sound was the American Bell X-1. On October 14, 1947, the bullet-shaped orange plane was dropped from a B-29 bomber. The X-1's pilot, Charles Yeager, fired its rocket engine and reached a speed of Mach 1.07. Yeager had become the first supersonic pilot.

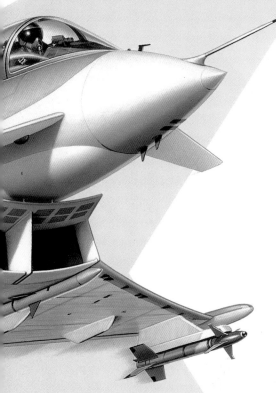

▼ Supersonic engines

Jet engines cannot work with air flowing through at supersonic speeds. Concorde has a special **channel** leading to the engine to slow down the air. Computer-controlled **ramps** move up and down to slow the speed of air from Mach 2 to only Mach 0.5.

▲ A drooping nose

Concorde's streamlined nose, or snout, is the best shape for flying faster than sound. However, it means that the pilot does not have a good view downward. As Concorde comes in to land, the nose tips down, or droops, so that the pilot can see the runway.

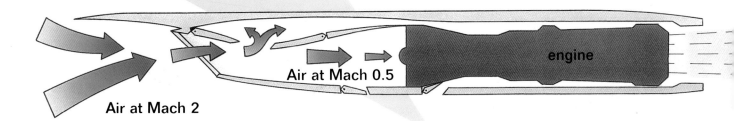

Air at Mach 0.5

engine

Air at Mach 2

Fast and Furious

Fighter planes are the fastest aircraft. Their job is to catch and attack enemy aircraft, so they must be quick and well armed. They have to be able to turn, climb, or dive at high speeds. The McDonnell Douglas F-15 Eagle is one of the world's top fighters. This amazing plane climbs at up to 820 feet (250 m) per second to a height of more than 60,000 feet (18,000 m). It flies at 1,650 miles per hour (2,655 kph), armed with a gun and up to eight **missiles**.

▲ Putting on weight
A fully armed fighter is much heavier than an unarmed plane, so it cannot fly at full speed. The missiles and **pylons** are all streamlined to cut down air resistance.

Swing-wing fighters
Straight wings are best for takeoff and landing, but swept back wings are better for high-speed flight. Swing-wing fighters have wings that swivel out for takeoff and landing, then swivel backward to form a delta wing for supersonic flight.

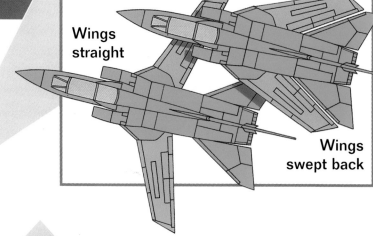

Wings straight

Wings swept back

**McDonnell Douglas
F-15 Eagle**

Straight up ➤
Fighter planes
are small aircraft
with enormous
engine power.
A fighter can fly
straight up, using
the huge force
of its engines to
overcome gravity.

**Vertical rolling
scissors**

◄ Dogfighting
Fighter pilots
use high-speed
twisting and
turning moves to
defend themselves.
In the scissors
maneuver and the
vertical rolling scissors,
pilots roll their aircraft as
each tries to get behind
the other and open fire.
Close air combat like this
is called a dogfight.

FAST FACTS
The Eurofighter has a talking
flight computer to help the
pilot **navigate**. The pilot
speaks to the computer,
and it speaks back!

Scissors

Flying to Win

The first air races were organized in the early days of flying to help develop faster aircraft. Air races are still held today for fun. Many racing planes are World War II fighters that have been rebuilt. A good racing plane is small and light, with a very powerful engine. Planes race against each other in fast and exciting contests.

P-38 Lightning

▲ First to Australia

In 1934 the first-ever air race from England to Australia took place. Three De Havilland DH-88 Comets were specially designed and built to take part. One of the Comets, called *Gloucester House*, won the race. It covered 11,330 miles (18,240 km) in 70 hours, 54 minutes at an average speed of 160 mph (256 kph).

▲ The Reno Air Races

Some of the best racing planes can be seen at the famous Reno Air Races. Many different kinds of aircraft participate, but the most exciting and popular events are the races for World War II planes. Every year these old warplanes are improved so that they fly even faster.

Racing over water

One of the most famous aircraft races was the Schneider Trophy seaplane race. Planes flew seven times around the 30-mile (48-km) route over the sea. The crowd watched from a nearby beach. The race route was marked by poles called pylons. The planes then flew around each pylon.

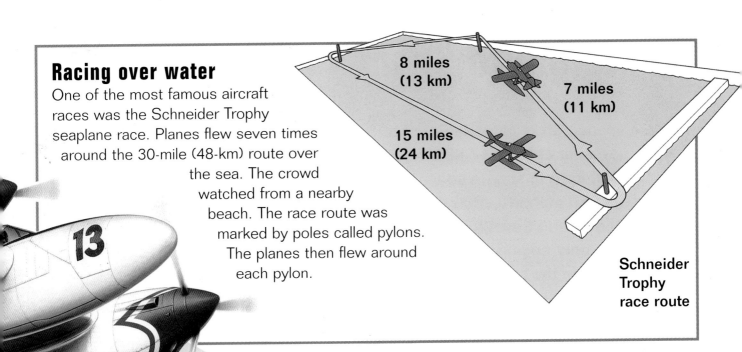

8 miles (13 km)

7 miles (11 km)

15 miles (24 km)

Schneider Trophy race route

P-51 Mustang

▼ Supermarine seaplanes

Seaplanes are aircraft that land on and take off from water. They have floats instead of wheels. The British Supermarine company built some of the most successful racing seaplanes. They won the Schneider Trophy race three times between 1927 and 1931. The Supermarine Spitfire was based on this winning design.

FAST FACTS

Just before a race, some planes are polished with an electric polisher. This reduces drag so that they can fly as fast as possible. It could just make the difference between winning and losing a race.

Blasting into Space

When a spacecraft is launched, it must reach a speed of at least 17,400 miles per hour (28,000 kph) to stay in space. If it reaches 24,850 mph (40,000 kph) it can leave the Earth and travel toward other planets. The only engine that has enough power for this is the rocket. A space shuttle has three rocket engines in its tail. They are supplied with fuel from a large, red tank attached to the shuttle. There are also two **booster rockets** that give the extra power needed for takeoff.

▲ Boosting the shuttle

At takeoff, booster rockets burn like huge fireworks. When the space shuttle reaches a height of 30 miles (50 km), the booster rockets fall into the Atlantic Ocean. They are collected by ships and refueled to launch another space shuttle.

Fuel tank falls away.

Boosters fall away.

Shuttle in space

Shuttle reenters atmosphere.

► Return to Earth

When a space shuttle reenters the atmosphere, it has to slow down from more than 20 times the speed of sound to 218 mph (350 kph) before it lands. It does this by flying along a zigzag path, slowing down all the time. It lands on a runway like an airliner.

Takeoff

Shuttle lands.

FAST FACTS

The space shuttle is covered with 27,000 glass tiles. They are specially designed to protect the shuttle and the crew inside from the incredible heat of reentry.

▶ Launching a rocket

Satellites are usually launched into space by rockets. A rocket is tall and slim with a bullet-shaped nose. It is powered through the atmosphere by motors in its tail. The rocket is controlled by computers, which make sure it stays on course.

Changing direction in space

A space shuttle has more than 40 tiny rocket **thrusters** in its nose and tail. They point in all directions and are fired to change the direction of the spacecraft. Two extra maneuvering engines in the tail are used to make bigger changes in speed and height.

Tail thrusters

Nose thrusters

Space shuttle

Spinning Wings

Helicopters are propelled through the air in a different way from aircraft with wings. Long, thin rotor blades spin above a helicopter and push air downward. This means that the helicopter takes off and lands vertically. The world speed helicopter record was set in 1986, when a British Westland Lynx reached 250 mph (400 kph). Even the fastest helicopters are slower than aircraft with wings, but new designs such as the Tiltrotor may change this.

▲ Super strength
The Sikorsky S-80 Super Stallion is one of the world's fastest and strongest helicopters. It has three powerful jet engines called **turboshafts** and a seven-bladed main rotor. It flies at a speed of 200 mph (315 kph).

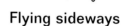

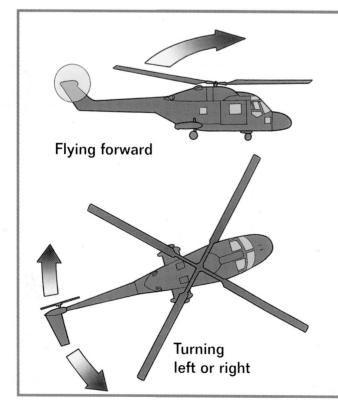

Flying forward

Turning left or right

Flying sideways

Steering and turning

To turn a helicopter from side to side, the pilot uses a control stick to lift the rotor blades on one side and lower them on the other. The blades can also be tilted down at the front and up at the back to move the helicopter forward. The small tail rotor helps the helicopter turn to the left or the right.

▼ Glass blades
Many modern helicopters have very strong rotor blades made from materials such as **carbon** and glass. The materials are mixed to strengthen each other. This mixture is called a **composite**.

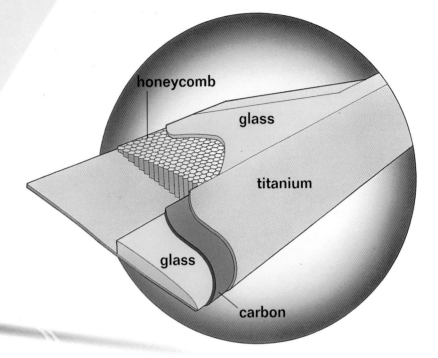

honeycomb

glass

titanium

glass

carbon

Westland Lynx

410

HMS GLOUCEST

Tilting rotors▶
The new Tiltrotor aircraft takes off vertically like a helicopter and then flies like an airplane. Long propellers lift it off the ground. Then the huge engines tilt forward and wings lift the aircraft. The Tiltrotor flies at twice the speed of an ordinary helicopter.

Bell Boeing

Staying in Control

A pilot steers an aircraft using controls in the cockpit. These are linked to parts of the wings and tail called control surfaces. When the control surfaces move, the air flowing around the plane presses against them. This makes the aircraft change direction. The fastest aircraft have computerized controls in the wings and tail because the force of air pressing against the surfaces is too strong for the pilot to move the controls by hand.

▲ Computers in the cockpit
Modern aircraft have computers that **monitor** the plane's speed, engines, and the surrounding sky. The computers are linked to screens in the cockpit.

▼ Control surfaces
There are three types of control surfaces. **Elevators** in the tail make the plane climb or dive. **Ailerons** in the wings make it roll. A **rudder** in the tail makes it turn left or right. Aircraft with a delta wing have panels in the wing called **elevons** that do the job of both elevators and ailerons.

McDonnell Douglas
F/A-18 Hornets

▲ Tumbling fighters
Some fighters are made unsteady so that they can turn, dive, and climb quickly. Computers make changes to the control surfaces many times every second to keep the plane flying smoothly. Many computerized fighters are used in exciting air displays.

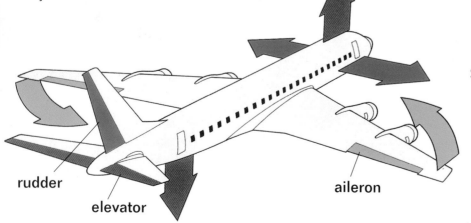

rudder

elevator

aileron

Heads-up
displays

Helmet-
mounted
display

▲ Making flying easier

A heads-up display projects flight
information onto a glass plate
in front of the pilot, so that
he or she doesn't have to look
down at computer screens.
Helmet-mounted displays are
now being developed. These
show information on the pilot's
visor to make it even easier to see.

▲ Formation flying

A fighter pilot must be
able to navigate well to stay
in control. Military aircraft fly in
tight **formations** to protect each
other. The clear **canopy** of this
Tornado GR1A gives the pilot a
good view of the other planes.

Record-Breakers

Some types of aircraft can reach amazing speeds. In 1967 the X-15 rocket plane flew at 4,520 mph (7,274 kph) when it was launched by being dropped from a B-52 bomber. When the space shuttle reenters the Earth's atmosphere, it travels at more than 15,535 mph (25,000 kph). The fastest aircraft to take off and land under its own power is the Lockheed SR-71 Blackbird. In 1976 it flew at 2,190 mph (3,529 kph) and set a new world air speed record.

The fastest airliner ➤
Concorde is still the world's fastest airliner. Only 20 were built, and only 12 are in regular service. They fly up to 100 passengers across the Atlantic Ocean at twice the speed of sound. This takes less than four hours.

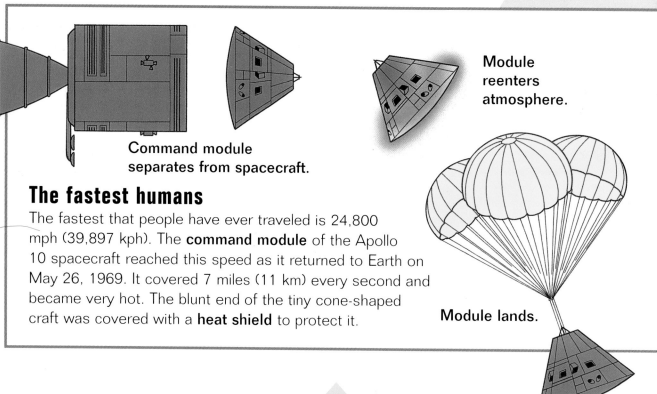

Command module separates from spacecraft.

Module reenters atmosphere.

The fastest humans

The fastest that people have ever traveled is 24,800 mph (39,897 kph). The **command module** of the Apollo 10 spacecraft reached this speed as it returned to Earth on May 26, 1969. It covered 7 miles (11 km) every second and became very hot. The blunt end of the tiny cone-shaped craft was covered with a **heat shield** to protect it.

Module lands.

**Lockheed
SR-71 Blackbird**

▲ Fastest in combat

The fastest combat aircraft is the Russian MiG-25. It flies at 2,050 mph (3,300 kph), faster than Mach 3. Most of the MiG-25 is made of steel. The nose and front edges of the wings are made of titanium, because they heat up so much in flight.

Above
2,500°F
(1,370°C)

Below
600°F
(315°C)

**◄ Super
hot!**

When the space shuttle reenters the Earth's atmosphere, it is traveling over ten times faster than Concorde. This diagram shows how hot the shuttle is at this speed. The lightest areas are the hottest.

◄ Top secret!

Lockheed SR-71 Blackbirds were once the United States' most successful spy planes. They carried out many top secret missions without ever being **intercepted**. Two are still used by **NASA** for high-speed, high-**altitude** research. They fly so fast that the front edges of the wings heat up to 806°F (430°C).

FAST FACTS

Charles Yeager became the world's first supersonic pilot in October 1947, even though he had two broken ribs at the time!

Shaping the Future

Designers are always working on faster aircraft for the future. Research centers and aircraft manufacturers around the world are developing aircraft that will replace Concorde. Scientists and engineers study ways of increasing engine power and speed, making better materials and cutting down on air pollution. As they find answers to these problems, amazing aircraft take shape on their computer screens.

➤ **Back-to-front wings**
One of the oddest-looking ideas for future fighters is to give them forward-swept wings. The wings are made from strong composite materials so that they do not break off during flight. The Grumman X-29 was built to test this idea.

◄ Faster than ever

Some designers are planning to build planes that can fly at speeds of more than Mach 5. These are called **hypersonic** aircraft. The body of the aircraft is shaped like one big wing, which makes it look very strange.

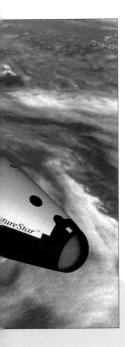

◄ A new Concorde

European aircraft manufacturers are working on a new supersonic aircraft that will be twice as fast as Concorde. It does not need a droop snout to help the pilot see the ground below. Instead, the pilot has a television screen in the cockpit that shows a clear view of the air space.

▲ Invisible aircraft

Some military aircraft are designed so that they do not show up on enemy radar screens. They are called stealth aircraft. The newest stealth fighter in the U.S. Air Force is the Lockheed Martin F-22. It zooms in on enemy planes without being seen.

➤ Future fighter

A new fighter aircraft for the 21st century is being developed in the United States. It is called the Joint Strike Fighter, and it will be faster and more difficult to spot on enemy **radar screens** than any other fighter. So far it only exists as a computer-generated picture.

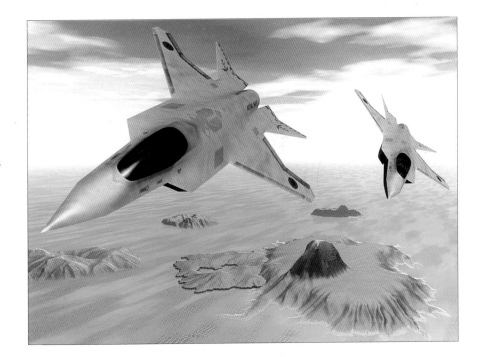

Glossary

acceleration
Going faster and faster.

afterburner
A part of a jet engine that sprays fuel into the hot gases coming out of the engine. This produces extra power.

ailerons
Movable panels in an aircraft wing. When one aileron lifts up, the aileron in the opposite wing moves down, and the plane rolls over to one side.

altitude
The height of an aircraft above the ground.

atmosphere
The gases that are all around the Earth or any other planet. We need these gases to live and breathe.

booster rocket
An extra rocket used to help launch a spacecraft. The space shuttle uses two booster rockets that fall away when their fuel runs out.

canopy
The see-through cover of an aircraft cockpit.

carbon
A black substance. Diamond, charcoal, and pencil leads are made of carbon. Carbon is used in building aircraft because it can be very strong and it does not melt at high temperatures.

cargo
Goods carried by a vehicle.

channel
A tube that gas or liquid flows through. A channel in Concorde's jet engine is shaped to slow down the air passing through it.

command module
The small, cone-shaped end of the Apollo spacecraft where the crew sits. When the astronauts return to Earth, the command module separates from the rest of the spacecraft and parachutes into the ocean.

composite
A material made from two or more different materials. A composite is very strong.

cruise
To fly at a steady speed. An aircraft's cruising speed is slower than its top speed.

delta wing
An aircraft wing swept back so far that it joins the body to make a triangular shape.

drag
Drag, or air resistance, is the force that slows an aircraft down.

elevators
Movable panels in an aircraft tail. When the elevators lift up, the tail drops, the nose rises, and the plane climbs. When the elevators move down, the nose drops and the plane dives.

elevons
Movable panels in the delta wing of a supersonic aircraft. They do the same job as elevators and ailerons on an ordinary aircraft.

formation
A group of aircraft flying together. Military planes fly in formation to protect each other.

fuselage
The main body of an aircraft.

gravity
A force that holds everything down on the ground. The heavier something is, the stronger its pull of gravity.

heat shield
The covering on a spacecraft that protects it from high temperatures.

hypersonic
Speeds of more than five times the speed of sound.

intercept
To keep enemy aircraft from reaching their target by sending fighters to catch them. These fighters are called interceptors.

maneuver
A controlled movement of an aircraft. A pilot has to be very skillful to carry out difficult maneuvers.

missile
A rocket-powered weapon that flies toward a target and explodes.

monitor
To check for problems or danger. Aircraft have computers to monitor the plane and the sky around it.

NASA
National Aeronautics and Space Administration. This is the organization that runs space projects in the United States.

navigate
To give directions for a plane. The member of the crew who does this is called the navigator. Modern aircraft use computers to navigate.

oxygen
A gas in the air around us. We need oxygen to breathe, and engines need oxygen to burn fuel.

propeller
Long blades that spin to push, or propel, an aircraft through the air.

pylon
The part of an aircraft that holds an engine or weapon in place underneath the plane.

radar screen
A screen that looks like a television screen or computer screen. It shows the positions of aircraft that are flying too far away for the pilot to see.

ramp
A sloping surface. Ramps in Concorde's engines move up and down to slow down air as it flows into the engine.

rudder
The part of an aircraft's tail that moves to the left or right to turn the aircraft from side to side.

satellite
An object that travels around and around a planet. The Earth's moon and moons that circle other planets are satellites. A spacecraft that travels around and around a planet is also called a satellite.

space shuttle
A spacecraft designed to be used again and again. It carries astronauts into space and back to Earth.

speed of sound
Sound travels through the air at about 760 mph (1,225 kph) near the ground. In colder air high above the ground, it falls to about 660 mph (1,062 kph). The speed of sound is also called Mach 1.

strut
A rod that holds aircraft parts in place.

supersonic
Faster than the speed of sound.

thrust
The force created by a propeller or an engine that pushes an aircraft forward.

thruster
A small rocket engine. It is used to make tiny changes to a spacecraft's position.

time zone
An area of the world that has a certain time. There are 24 time zones in the world. If you travel from one time zone to another, you have to change your watch because the time changes.

titanium
A strong, light metal. It is used to make fast aircraft.

turbine
Part of a jet engine. A turbine is a disk with blades around the edge. As hot gases rush through a jet engine, they hit the blades and make the turbine spin.

turboshaft
A helicopter engine. It is connected to a shaft, or rod, that turns the rotor blades.

undercarriage
An aircraft's wheels.

visor
The see-through part of a helmet that covers a pilot's face.

weld
To join two pieces of metal or plastic by melting them together.

wind tunnel
A tunnel with a strong wind flowing through it. A model of a new aircraft is placed inside a wind tunnel. Designers watch how the model moves in the wind to find out how the real aircraft will fly.

Index

acceleration 7, 30
afterburner 7, 30
aileron 24, 30
air display 24
airliners 4, 5, 6, 7, 12, 20, 26
air pollution 28
air races 18, 19
air resistance 6, 7, 8, 14, 16
air speed record 12, 26
Apollo 10 26
atmosphere 13, 20, 21, 26, 27

BAe Hawk 200 8
Bell X-1 14–15
Boeing 747 5, 10, 11
Boeing 767 6
booster rocket 20, 30
Bower, Ron 23

canopy 25, 30
carbon 23, 30
cockpit 9, 24, 29
command module 26, 30
composite 23, 30
computer-aided design 8
computers 8, 9, 10, 11, 15, 21, 24, 25, 28
Concorde 5, 7, 12, 15, 26, 27, 28, 29
control surfaces 24

Dash 7 6
Dassault Rafale 6, 7
De Havilland Comets 5, 18
delta wing 6, 14, 16, 24, 30
dogfighting 17
Douglas DC-3 4
drag 6, 8, 19, 30

early planes 7, 11, 18
ejection seat 9
elevator 24, 30
elevon 24, 30

engine 7, 8, 10, 12, 13, 14, 15, 17, 18, 20, 21, 22, 23, 28
Eurofighter 14, 17

fighter aircraft 4, 6, 7, 12, 16, 17, 18, 24, 25, 28
flying test bed 10
formations 25, 30
fuel 7, 12, 13, 14, 20
fuselage 6, 30

gravity 8, 17, 30

heads-up display 25
heat shield 26, 30
helicopters 22, 23
helmet-mounted display 25
hypersonic aircraft 28–29, 30

jet aircraft 5, 6, 7, 12
jet engine 7, 12, 13, 15, 22
Joint Strike Fighter 29

Lockheed Martin F-22 10–11, 29
Lockheed SR-71 Blackbird 26, 27

Mach numbers 11
McDonnell Douglas F/A-18 Hornet 24, 25
McDonnell Douglas F-15 Eagle 11, 16, 17
Messerschmitt Me-163 Komet 12
MiG-25 27
missiles 16, 30

NASA 27, 31
navigating 17, 25, 31

P-38 Lightning 18–19
P-51 Mustang 18–19
piston engine 7
propeller 11, 23, 31
pylon 16, 31

radar screen 29, 31
ramjet 13

Reno Air Races 18
rocket 9, 12, 13, 21
rocket engine 13, 15, 20, 21
rotor blades 22, 23
rudder 24, 31

satellite 21, 31
Schneider Trophy 19
seaplanes 19
Sepecat Jaguar 11
Sikorsky S-80 Super Stallion 22
sonic boom 14
spacecraft 20, 21, 26
space shuttle 10, 13, 20, 21, 26, 27, 31
speed of sound 4, 11, 14, 20, 26, 31
spy plane 27
stealth aircraft 29
streamlining 6, 7, 14, 15, 16
Supermarine seaplane 19
Supermarine Spitfire 4, 19
supersonic aircraft 5, 6, 14, 15, 16, 27, 29, 31
swing-wing fighters 16

thrust 8, 31
thruster 21, 31
Tiltrotor 22, 23
time zone 15, 31
titanium 9, 23, 27, 31
Tornado 12, 25
turbine 13, 31
turbofan 12, 13
turbojet 12, 13

undercarriage 6, 31

visor 25, 31

Westland Lynx 22, 23
wind tunnel 11, 31
World War I 4
World War II 4, 18
Wright Flyer 4